The Fabulous, Freaky, Unusual History of PRO WRESTLING

BY ANGIE PETERSON KAELBERER

Content Consultant: Mike Johnson,
Writer, PWInsider.com

CAPSTONE PRESS
a capstone imprint

Velocity is published by Capstone Press,
151 Good Counsel Drive, P.O. Box 669, Mankato, Minnesota 56002.
www.capstonepub.com

Books published by Capstone Press are manufactured with paper
containing at least 10 percent post-consumer waste.

Library of Congress Cataloging-in-Publication Data
Kaelberer, Angie Peterson.
 The fabulous, freaky, unusual history of pro wrestling / by Angie Peterson Kaelberer.
   p. cm. – (Unusual histories)
 Includes bibliographical references and index.
 ISBN 978-1-4296-4789-2 (library binding)
 1. Wrestling—History. 2. Wrestling—United States—History. I. Title.
 II. Series.
  GV1195.K214 2011
  796.812—dc22   2010014596

Editorial Credits
Editor: Brenda Haugen
Designer: Veronica Correia
Media Researcher: Wanda Winch
Production Specialist: Eric Manske

Photo Credits
AP Images: B. Vartan Boyajian, 36; Corbis: Bettmann, 7 (bottom right), 32, Reuters/Mario Anzuoni, 45 (top),
Sygma/Kraig Geiger, 34; Courtesy of Figures Toy Company, 19 (top); Getty Images, Inc: Bill Olive, 4, Bruce
Bennett Studios, 17, Focus on Sport, 33 (top), Gaye Gerard, cover, 8, Sean Gallup, 42, WireImage/Bob Levey,
14 (The Undertaker), 27, WireImage/Don Arnold, 35 (top); Globe Photos: Allstar/Graham Whitby-Boot,
10-11, 18; iStockphoto: vid64, 31; Library of Congress: Prints and Photographs Division, 6; Shutterstock:
3drenderings, 37 (middle), Alexander Kalina, 33 (bottom), angel digital, 37 (bottom), ARENA creative, 24-25
(top), Barauskaite, 14-15 (flame bkgrnd), Chris Anderson, 19 (bottom), clearviewstock, 30-31 (bkgrnd), Dario
Sabljak, 6 (television), 7 (television), 38 (flag), David Mingay, 31, Denis Nata, 22-23 (top), Eky Studio (metal
bolt background), Filip Fuxa, 13 (snake bkgrnd), fivespots, 13 (snake), fotosav, 21 (bottom), Hywit Dimyadi,
25 (bottom), ilker canikligil, 32-35 (bkgrnd), James Steidl, 26-27 (bkgrnd), 40 (top), Jana Guothova, 32-35
(tickets), JM-Design, 20-21 (back), Johny Keny, 35 (bottom left), kahramaninsan, 23 (bottom), Karlionau, 16,
mariait, 14-15 (fire icon), Markus Gann, 44 (bottom right), monared, 44 (top), Mordechai Meiri, 28 (top),
Natutik, 14-15 (flame strip), oxygen64, 32 (top), Pakhnyushcha, 38 (bottom), Pavel K, 12 (music notes),
Petar Milevski, 25 (top), Rafa Irusga, 44 (bottom left), Robert Adrian Hillman, 37 (top), Salim October, 9
(fist), Sergey Prygov, 28 (bottom), Sergey Shlyaev, 12-13 (wall and door), sergwsq, 45 (bottom), sgame, 11
(ladder), Stawek, 39 (top), Thank You, 29 (bottom), Unholy Vault Designs, 38 (back), Valeria Pol, 35 (bottom
right); Sports Legends Photos, Inc., 12 (Gorgeous George); Yesterday's Classics: The Baldwin Online Children's
Literature Project, www.mainlesson.com, 5; Wrealano@aol.com, 20, 22, 23 (middle), 24, 26, 29 (top), 30, 39

TABLE OF CONTENTS

Chapter 1

A Wild Ride

From Carnivals to Stadiums

On April 5, 2009, nearly 73,000 people crowded into Reliant Stadium in Houston, Texas.

Why were they there? Was it the Super Bowl? No! But the fans were there to see the Super Bowl of pro wrestling—WWE's WrestleMania.

Today, people all over the world watch pro wrestling live and on TV. But most wrestling fans probably don't know that in the United States, pro wrestling has been around for more than 100 years.

Famous Matches of 2009 WrestleMania:

Chris Jericho vs. WWE Legends

Edge vs. John Cena vs. Big Show

Jeff Hardy vs. Matt Hardy

Shawn Michaels vs. Undertaker

Rey Mysterio vs. JBL

Randy Orton vs. Triple H

● winners

Chris Jericho

73,000 screaming fans

Ric Flair

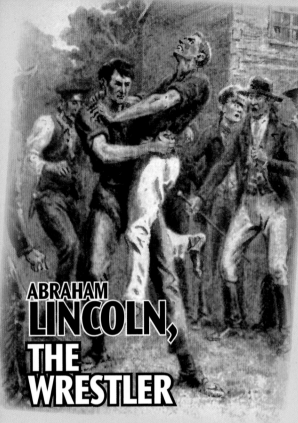

ABRAHAM LINCOLN, THE WRESTLER

Everyone knows Abraham Lincoln was a U.S. president. But did you know he also was a pro wrestler? Historians believe he wrestled about 300 matches. His most famous match was in 1831, when he was 22. Lincoln wrestled a bully named Jack Armstrong. Lincoln won the match by lifting Armstrong and shaking him like a rag.

In the late 1800s, carnival strongmen began challenging the public to wrestle. They would call to men as they walked by and dare them to show off their strength in a match. In time, strongmen started wrestling one another. People loved it!

In the 1930s, carnivals traveled the country and put on small wrestling shows. By the mid-1940s, the shows were growing larger.

Pro wrestling has come a long way from those humble beginnings. Today, it's a huge business with fans worldwide. But how did it get there?

Ed "Strangler" Lewis

Ivan Linow

In the early 1900s, wrestling promoters started staging matches in city theaters and arenas. But wrestling still wasn't known all over the United States.

That began to change, thanks to an invention created by Philo Farnsworth.

In 1927, he demonstrated the first working TV system. Twelve years later, fans watched a wrestling match on TV for the first time. Few people owned TV sets then, but after World War II (1939–1945), they became popular.

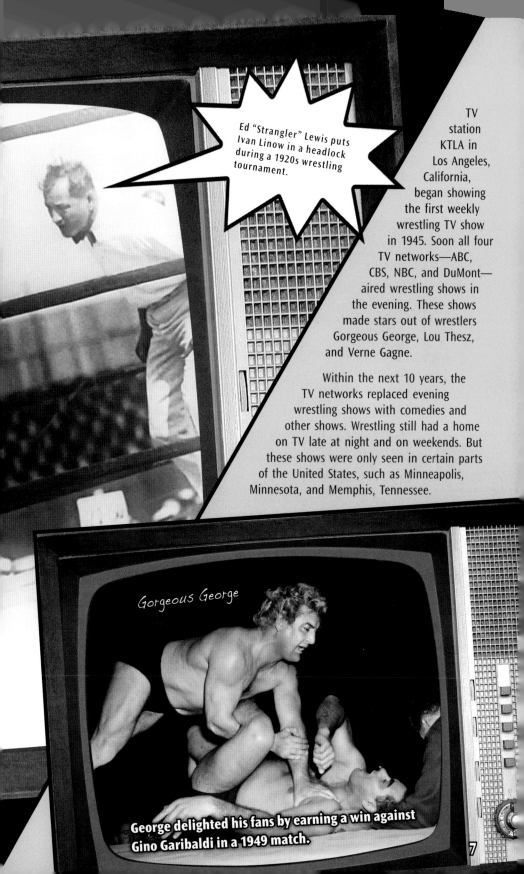

Ed "Strangler" Lewis puts Ivan Linow in a headlock during a 1920s wrestling tournament.

TV station KTLA in Los Angeles, California, began showing the first weekly wrestling TV show in 1945. Soon all four TV networks—ABC, CBS, NBC, and DuMont— aired wrestling shows in the evening. These shows made stars out of wrestlers Gorgeous George, Lou Thesz, and Verne Gagne.

Within the next 10 years, the TV networks replaced evening wrestling shows with comedies and other shows. Wrestling still had a home on TV late at night and on weekends. But these shows were only seen in certain parts of the United States, such as Minneapolis, Minnesota, and Memphis, Tennessee.

Gorgeous George

George delighted his fans by earning a win against Gino Garibaldi in a 1949 match.

In the early 1980s, cable TV changed all that. Cable stations brought wrestling shows to fans all over the country. Major events were seen on pay-per-view (PPV). Wrestling shows on cable TV remain popular today.

Every week, WWE fans can watch a live show called *Raw*. They also can see taped shows, such as *SmackDown* and *Superstars*.

1950s: By the 1950s, the United States was divided into wrestling territories. Each territory controlled wrestling events in its area. Each area often had a local TV show. Territory owners agreed not to put on shows in another owner's territory without permission. Territories were organized into companies.

FACT: Former wrestler The Rock gave SmackDown its name. He often threatened to "lay the smackdown" on his opponents.

Undertaker

Kane

Chavo Guerrero Jr.

Bam Neely

Great Khali

Undertaker and Kane stare down Bam Neely, Chavo Guerrero Jr., and Great Khali during a 2008 SmackDown match. The event was one of five SmackDown stops in an Australian tour in 2008.

pay-per-view—a cable or satellite TV service that allows customers to watch a special event for a fee

PRO WRESTLING COMPANIES
BASH IT OUT

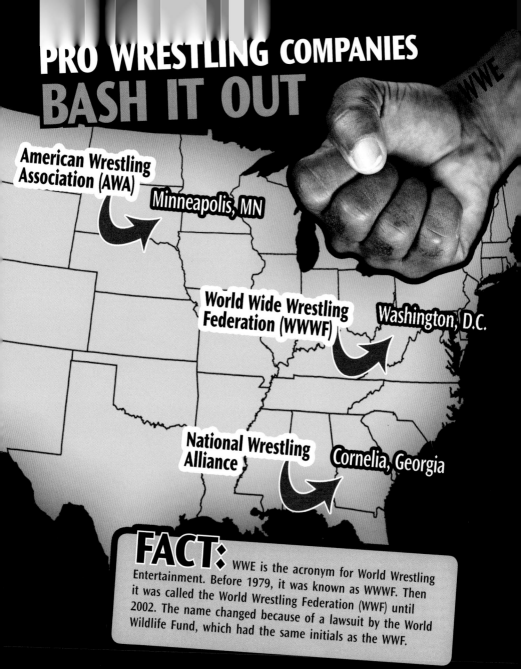

American Wrestling Association (AWA)

Minneapolis, MN

World Wide Wrestling Federation (WWWF)

Washington, D.C.

National Wrestling Alliance

Cornelia, Georgia

WWE

FACT: WWE is the acronym for World Wrestling Entertainment. Before 1979, it was known as WWWF. Then it was called the World Wrestling Federation (WWF) until 2002. The name changed because of a lawsuit by the World Wildlife Fund, which had the same initials as the WWF.

1980s: By the 1980s, WWE had bought many smaller companies. It became the major U.S. wrestling company. WWE's main rival was World Championship Wrestling (WCW).

Today: WWE is still the biggest company today. However, it has competition from the NWA, Total Nonstop Action Wrestling (TNA), and Ring of Honor (ROH).

territory—an area that is controlled by one wrestling promoter who charges people money to watch an event

Chapter 2

Just the Basics

Playing by the Rules?

Chris Benoit

Kane

The ring-rope rule applies when a wrestler is caught in an opponent's hold. If the wrestler gets under or on the ring ropes, his opponent has to release him before the referee counts to five.

Pro wrestling matches sometimes seem like free-for-alls. But the sport really does have rules. These rules often change from match to match.

Weapons are supposed to be off-limits, but this rule is often ignored. Wrestlers are not usually disqualified for using weapons.

Some matches are even built around the use of weapons. These include Tables, Ladders, and Chairs (TLC) matches. TLC matches trace their start to ladder matches. In a ladder match, an item is hung over a ladder. The first wrestler to climb the ladder and retrieve the item is the winner.

A 1972 battle in which Dan Kroffat defeated Tor Kamata in Alberta, Canada, may have been the first ladder match.

Famous TLC matches:

Jeff Hardy vs. **CM Punk** (2009)

Edge vs. Chris Benoit vs. Shelton Benjamin vs. Chris Jericho vs. Christian vs. Kane (2005)

Edge and Christian vs. the Hardy Boyz vs. the Dudley Boyz (2001)

Edge and Christian vs. the Hardy Boyz vs. the Dudley Boyz (2000)

● winners

FACT◆ Ladders
used in TLC matches often are more than twice as tall as the wrestlers. There is no rule saying how big the ladder must be. However, they usually are 16 feet (4.9 meters) tall.

Wrestlers play roles during their matches. They can be heels or babyfaces. Most wrestlers also create characters. These in-ring personalities often involve costumes, makeup, and catchphrases that they shout at their opponents or the fans. Through history, wrestlers also have had gimmicks, which are clever tricks or ideas used to get people's attention.

In the 1940s, Gorgeous George created pro wrestling's first major character. George's character revolved around his looks. George was a heel. He loved annoying the fans. Angry fans sometimes even attacked him!

George was one of the first to use entrance music. "Pomp and Circumstance" always played as he made his way to the ring.

Gorgeous George

heel—a wrestler who acts as a villain in the ring
babyface—a wrestler who acts as a hero in the ring

George bleached his curly hair blond. His hairstyle even had a name—the Marcel. He called the gold bobby pins that held his hair in place "Georgie pins."

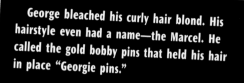

Gorgeous George

George's assistants sprayed the air around him with perfume. George called it Chanel #10.

George walked to the ring wearing long robes. The robes had different styles. Some were frilly. Others were elegant. George had more than 100 robes.

FACT:

Jake "The Snake" Roberts had an unusual gimmick too. He carried his pet python, Damien, into the ring with him. After Jake won a match, he dropped Damien onto the opponent's body.

Undertaker is one of the longest-running characters in WWE history. He started wrestling in the late 1980s. He joined WWE in 1990 as the Undertaker. In the 1880s, funeral directors were called undertakers. Undertaker dressed like he was from that time. Undertaker's character changed a bit in the early 2000s. He became a tough biker. But soon he was back to the familiar spooky character that audiences loved.

Rest in peace!

As Undertaker walks to the ring, creepy organ music plays.

Undertaker

Undertaker makes an entrance as fire explodes. One time, this entrance got him into trouble. In February 2010, a fireball exploded too close to him. Undertaker suffered minor burns on his chest. But the show went on.

Undertaker's black leather jacket has changed little over the years. Now he wears a black tank top underneath it. At one time though, he wore a vest.

Top 10 Catchphrases Throughout History

1
"Whatcha gonna do, brother, when Hulkamania runs wild on you?"
Hulk Hogan

2
"And that's the bottom line, because Stone Cold says so!"
"Stone Cold" Steve Austin

3
"Do you smell what The Rock is cooking?"
The Rock

4
"To be the man, you gotta beat the man!"
Ric Flair

5
"Have a nice day!"
Mick Foley

6
"Rest in peace!"
Undertaker

7
"Ohhh yeah, dig it!"
"Macho Man" Randy Savage

8
"The best there is, the best there was, and the best there ever will be."
Bret "Hit Man" Hart

9
"D-Von! Get the tables!"
The Dudley Boyz

10
"You pencilneck geek!"
"Classy" Freddie Blassie

Undertaker sometimes fought matches where he would shut his opponent into a casket. In one match, Undertaker wrestled Kane in a ring surrounded by fire. Undertaker won the match by putting Kane's arm in the fire.

Gimmick
Matches

Wrestlers don't just have gimmicks as part of their characters. Throughout history, they have also wrestled in gimmick matches. These matches have special rules and conditions that make them exciting for fans to watch.

Royal Rumble

In Royal Rumble matches, a large group of wrestlers draws numbers to decide the order they will enter the ring. Every 90 seconds, another wrestler enters the ring. If a wrestler is tossed out or falls out of the ring onto the floor, he's eliminated. The last wrestler left in the ring is the winner. WWE's Royal Rumble event has been held each year since 1988.

Royal Rumble
Records

Most wins: "Stone Cold" Steve Austin has three (1997, 1998, 2001).

Longest time in a Royal Rumble: In 2006, Rey Mysterio stayed in the ring for 1 hour, 2 minutes, and 12 seconds.

Shortest time in a Royal Rumble: In 2009, Santino Marella was thrown from the ring in just 1.9 seconds.

First woman in a Royal Rumble: Chyna (1999)

Luckiest number: 27. The wrestler drawing this number has won four times. No other number has had more winners.

All Locked Up

During cage or cell matches, the ring is inside a 16-foot (4.9-m) cage. After the cage door is locked, no one is supposed to get in or out until one wrestler defeats the other. It doesn't always work that way, though. In one of the most famous cell matches, Mankind and Undertaker were battling on top of the cell roof. Undertaker used a chokeslam to hurl Mankind though the metal mesh roof.

Ivan
Koloff

The
Warlord

Road
Warrior
Animal

16 feet

$tepping UP

For many wrestling fans, ladder matches are among the most exciting events. The action is nonstop as wrestlers fight to be the first to climb the ladder and claim the prize.

Kane

Chris Jericho

FACT:

A ladder match gives a wrestler a chance to show off his high-flying skills. Wrestlers often use the ladder to launch acrobatic attacks on their opponents.

WrestleMania 21 featured a Money in the Bank Ladder Match. In the match, Edge defeated Chris Benoit, Chris Jericho, Kane, Christian, and Shelton Benjamin to claim the cash.

That "prize" is usually a championship belt. It also can be a suitcase full of money, a wrestling contract, or almost anything else.

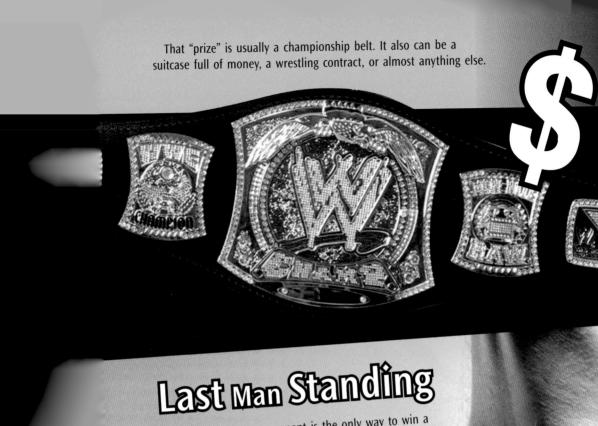

Last Man Standing

Knocking out an opponent is the only way to win a Last Man Standing match. If a wrestler is knocked down and can't stand before the referee counts to 10, his opponent wins.

One of the most exciting Last Man Standing matches happened in 2007. It involved John Cena and Umaga in a battle for the WWE Championship. They used all their tricks. They hurled steel steps at each other. They even destroyed a ringside table!

Finally a bloody Cena untied the top ring rope. He used it to choke his opponent. At last the huge Umaga passed out. Cena was the winner.

They Have the Moves

Besides characters and catchphrases, wrestlers have their own finishing moves. These moves include different types of holds, pins, bodyslams, and aerial moves. Some of these moves are similar. But they all have something that makes them unique to that particular wrestler. Finishing moves have been part of wrestling since the beginning. In fact, many of today's moves are based off moves created in the past.

In the 1950s, Karl Gotch, who was part German, inspired the German suplex. Gotch stood behind his opponent and lifted him up by the waist. He then fell backward, slamming the opponent's shoulders to the mat.

Jake the Snake

FACT: Some wrestlers became so famous for particular moves that they are named after them. Lou Thesz wrestled from the 1930s until he retired in 1990 at age 74. For his finishing move, Thesz knocked over his opponent. Then he sat on his opponent's chest, pinning him to the mat with his legs. This move is called the Lou Thesz press.

aerial move—a wrestling move that is done off the ropes or a high object, such as a ladder

DDT:

Pick Your Poison

About 30 years after the German suplex was invented, Jake "The Snake" Roberts created the DDT. It was named after a type of poison. Jake put his opponent in a front facelock. Then he fell backward, smashing his opponent's head into the ring. Today wrestlers have come up with at least 25 versions of the DDT.

In an **elevated** DDT, a wrestler puts his opponent on an elevated surface, usually the ropes or a turnbuckle. At the same time, he applies a front facelock.

A **jumping** DDT is similar to a regular DDT. But instead of just falling backward, a wrestler jumps up while holding his opponent in a front facelock.

During a **flip** DDT, the wrestler holds his opponent in a front facelock. Then the wrestler pushes off the mat with his legs, flips his opponent, and drives him onto the top of his head.

During a **spinning** DDT, a wrestler goes to the top rope and puts his opponent in a front facelock. Then the wrestler jumps forward, spins halfway around to fall backward, and drops his opponent's head onto the mat.

MAKING OLD MOVES NEW

Hakushi

Other wrestlers take established moves and make them their own. Chris Jericho does a version of the Boston crab. He calls it the Walls of Jericho. Jericho turns his opponent facedown and grabs both of his legs. He then bends the opponent's legs back toward the opponent's face. Triple H's Pedigree move is based on the double underhook facebuster. Triple H holds his opponent facedown and drops to his knees, slamming his opponent's head to the mat.

The Tall and Short of It

Wrestling is a sport that is full of extremes—from the action on the mat to the personalities outside the ring. Wrestlers' bodies are extreme too. Some are very large or rippling with muscles. Throughout its history, the sport also includes extremes in heights. Success can be found in the ring for the shortest and tallest of wrestlers.

Hornswoggle was the first little person to win a WWE championship. He won the Cruiserweight Championship at the Great American Bash July 22, 2007. Just 21 years old, he was the youngest, shortest, and lightest man to ever win the title.

At 5 feet, 10 inches (178 centimeters), Fit Finlay was an average-sized wrestler, but he towered over Hornswoggle.

Matt Hardy (right) sometimes joined the tag team of Fit Finlay and Hornswoggle.

Matt Hardy

At 4 feet, 5 inches (135 cm) and 115 pounds (52 kg), Hornswoggle was among the smallest wrestlers in history. He joined the WWE in 2006. He often teamed with Dave "Fit" Finlay.

Fit Finlay

Hornswoggle

cruiserweight—a wrestling class in which wrestlers weigh no more than 215 pounds (97.5 kg)

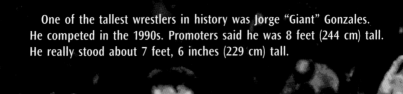
One of the tallest wrestlers in history was Jorge "Giant" Gonzales. He competed in the 1990s. Promoters said he was 8 feet (244 cm) tall. He really stood about 7 feet, 6 inches (229 cm) tall.

Jorge "Giant" Gonzales

Already a giant of a man, Gonzales went to extremes when choosing his costume. He wore a full-body suit that had muscles painted on it. The suit even had hair!

FACT:

In 1988, Gonzales competed in the Olympics as part of Argentina's basketball team. He was drafted that same year by the Atlanta Hawks, a pro basketball team. At the time, he was believed to be the world's tallest basketball player.

The Big Events

Every week, fans can watch wrestling shows for free on TV. But once a month or so, wrestling companies pull out all the stops for their PPV events. These shows feature several major matches between the biggest stars.

WrestleMania is the granddaddy of all wrestling PPVs. WWE held the first WrestleMania March 31, 1985, at Madison Square Garden in New York City. The event did so well that WWE decided to continue it every year.

Andre the Giant

Big John Studd

Famous Matches of
1985 WrestleMania:

Hulk Hogan and Mr. T vs. Rowdy Roddy Piper and "Mr. Wonderful" Paul Orndorff

Leilani Kai vs. Wendi Richter

Special Delivery Jones vs. King Kong Bundy

The Executioner vs. Tito Santana

Andre the Giant vs. Big John Studd

Greg "The Hammer" Valentine vs. Junkyard Dog

● winners

PPV events also include lots of fireworks and other special effects. Sometimes famous actors or rock bands appear too.

FACT:
Many celebrities joined the wild wrestling fans at WrestleMania 1. Among them were boxer Muhammad Ali, singer Cyndi Lauper, baseball great Billy Martin, and flashy musician Liberace.

FAMOUS PPV FIRSTS OF THE WWE

January 1998
Royal Rumble

February 1998
Elimination Chamber*

March 1985
WrestleMania

April 1999
Backlash

May 2005
Extreme Rules

June 2008
Night of Champions

August 1988
SummerSlam

October 1997
Hell in a Cell

October 2009
Bragging Rights

November 1987
Survivor Series

December 2009
TLC

*Called "No Way Out" until 2010

All the WrestleManias have been entertaining, but a few were unforgettable.

Wrestle Mania 3

At WrestleMania 3 in 1987, Hulk Hogan defeated Andre the Giant by bodyslamming him. During his career, Andre rarely was bodyslammed. WrestleMania 3 marked the first time it happened to Andre in front of a national audience.

Andre the Giant

Hulk Hogan

Andre the Giant stood 7 feet (213 cm) tall. He weighed anywhere from 300 pounds (136 kg) to more than 500 pounds (227 kg) during his career. He often made his opponents look like ragdolls as he lifted them over his head. Rarely were they able to do the same to him.

Wrestle Mania 12

At WrestleMania 12 in 1996, Shawn Michaels and Bret Hart gave the crowd its money's worth. They wrestled for an hour in an Iron Man match for the World Heavyweight title. The two superstars went into overtime to determine a winner. About two minutes into overtime, Michaels used his finishing move, Sweet Chin Music. He won the match and the title.

Wrestle Mania 25

Shawn Michaels

Undertaker

Michaels was also part of another famous WrestleMania match. At WrestleMania 25 in 2009, he fought Undertaker. Right from the start, it seemed like a battle between good and evil. Michaels emerged from a cloud of white smoke and was lowered onto a stage. He entered the ring dressed in white. Undertaker rose up from beneath the stage. As usual, he wore all black.

The two wrestlers stalked each other around the ring. Michaels nearly defeated his opponent. But Undertaker fought back for the win.

FACT: Undertaker holds a WrestleMania record. Since 1991, he's wrestled 18 WrestleMania matches. He has won them all! No other wrestler even comes close to his winning record.

Life as a Wrestler

Teaming Up

Wrestlers don't always enter the ring alone. Tag teams and stables have been part of wrestling since the early days. Pairing up two wrestlers to form a tag team started in the 1930s. When two tag teams wrestle, one member of the team is in the ring. If the wrestler in the ring has had enough, he slaps, or "tags," his teammate's hand. The teammate then jumps into the ring.

Fabulous Kangaroos

The Fabulous Kangaroos tag team formed in Australia in 1957. Al Costello and Roy Heffernan were the original members. Their gimmick was tossing boomerangs into the audience. They won three WWE U.S. Tag Team titles. After Costello and Heffernan retired, other wrestlers kept the Kangaroos going until 1983.

stable—group of wrestlers who protect one another during matches and sometimes wrestle together

Midnight Rockers

Marty Jannetty

Shawn Michaels

Shawn Michaels and Marty Jannetty teamed up to form the Midnight Rockers in 1985. They won two tag team championships in the American Wrestling Association (AWA). In 1986, they joined WWE as the Rockers. They were one of the most popular tag teams of the 1980s. They won many matches. However, they never managed to win the WWE World Tag Team Championship.

In early 1992, the Rockers split up. Michaels went on to huge success as a singles wrestler.

Jannetty also continued wrestling, but never with the popularity that he had with the Rockers.

Dudley Boyz

Bubba Ray and D-Von Dudley weren't really brothers, but their characters in the Dudley Boyz were. The Dudleys formed in the late 1990s in Extreme Championship Wrestling (ECW). They joined WWE in 2000. During their time in the ECW, they won eight tag team titles. Their finishing move was the Dudley Death Drop, where they slammed opponents to the floors of wrestling rings.

Hardy Boyz

Unlike the Dudley Boyz, the Hardy Boyz really are brothers. Matt Hardy and his younger brother Jeff grew up wrestling in their backyard in Cameron, North Carolina. They joined WWE in 1998 when Matt was 23 and Jeff was 20. Their tattoos, piercings, and dyed hair soon gave them the nickname "Team Extreme."

Jeff Hardy

Michael Hayes

Matt Hardy

nWo New World Order

WCW was the home of a popular heel stable known as New World Order (nWo). In 1996, "Hollywood" Hulk Hogan turned heel. He teamed with Scott Hall and Kevin Nash to form nWo. Syxx, The Giant, and Buff Bagwell soon joined them.

Members took down other wrestlers, spray-painting "nWo" on their backs. The nWo continued to terrify WCW until breaking up in 2000.

D-Generation X

In 1997, WWE got its own heel stable, D-Generation X (DX). Triple H, Shawn Michaels, Chyna, and Rick Rude were the original DX members. X-Pac, RoadDogg, and Billy Gunn joined them later. DX used sarcasm to poke fun at other wrestlers. DX broke up in 2000. Michaels and Triple H later reunited as a DX tag team.

FACT:
DX members loved playing pranks. They even drove an army vehicle to rival company WCW's event in Atlanta, Georgia.

Women
in Wrestling

Women have been part of pro wrestling since the early days. Often they work as managers or **valets** for male wrestlers. But many have had careers of their own inside the ring.

One Tough Lady

In the 1930s, Mildred Burke started her career by wrestling men at carnivals. Burke claimed to have won at least 150 matches against men.

Mildred
Burke

Burke later switched to wrestling women. She held the NWA Women's World title from 1935 to 1954. She later formed her own women's wrestling company.

105034061

valet—a person who walks to the ring with a wrestler and helps the wrestler during matches

Many fans consider the Fabulous Moolah the greatest female wrestler ever. She started her career in the late 1940s as a valet for wrestlers Buddy Rogers and the Elephant Boy.

In 1956 she beat 13 other women to become the NWA Women's World Champion. She held the title for most of the next 30 years.

Best of the Best?

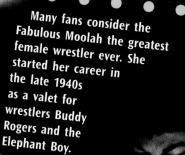

Moolah

In 1972, Moolah became the first woman permitted to wrestle at Madison Square Garden in New York City. She won the WWE Women's Championship in 1999. She was 76 years old at the time! Moolah continued to appear on WWE TV shows until shortly before her death in 2007.

FACT: When young Moolah was asked why she wanted to wrestle, she replied she was doing it "for the moolah!" That remark gave Moolah her wrestling name.

In the 1970s and 1980s, women mainly returned to working as managers and valets. But in the late 1990s, one woman changed all that.

Chyna was 5 feet, 10 inches (178 cm), and 180 pounds (82 kg) of pure muscle! She trained as a bodybuilder before getting into wrestling. Chyna started in the WWE as a bodyguard for Triple H.

Chyna paved the way for other athletic female wrestlers such as Lita, Ivory, Molly Holly, and Trish Stratus.

The Rock

Chyna

Chyna became a member of DX and wrestled both men and women. In 1999, she defeated Jeff Jarrett to become the only female Intercontinental Champion. She competed in the Royal Rumble and won the WWE Women's Championship before leaving the company in 2001.

Today's female wrestlers, called divas, are known more for their beauty than for their wrestling abilities. But top divas such as Melina, Mickie James, and Michelle McCool have managed to win the WWE Women's Championship.

Psycho Diva

Victoria

Michelle McCool

Michelle McCool flies at Victoria during a June 2008 SmackDown showdown in Australia. McCool was a middle-school teacher before becoming a wrestling diva.

FACT: Lita won the WWE Women's Championship four times in her seven-year career. She retired from wrestling in 2006 and is now the lead singer of a punk rock band called The Luchagors.

Famous Feuds

Feuds between wrestlers have been part of the sport since the beginning. Wrestlers often argue with one another in and out of the ring. Some feuds go on for months or even years.

At one time in the 1980s, Hulk Hogan and "Macho Man" Randy Savage were friends. They helped each other during matches. They even formed a tag team called the Mega Powers. But jealousy began to eat away at their friendship. Savage's manager, Elizabeth, became Hogan's manager too. Savage didn't like how close Hogan and Elizabeth were getting.

Hulk Hogan earned $1.8 million and the World Championship title after defeating Randy Savage at WrestleMania 5.

Hulk Hogan

By 1989, tensions between the two wrestlers carried over into the ring. During a tag team match with the Twin Towers, Savage attacked Hogan with the World Championship belt. Hogan then challenged Savage to a match for the World Championship title at WrestleMania. Hogan won the match and the title, but the feud continued. Unable to work together, Mega Powers split up. The feud finally ended in 1990 when Hogan defeated Savage at the Main Event.

feud—long-running quarrel

One of the biggest feuds of the 1990s involved Bret "Hitman" Hart and Shawn Michaels.

After this match, things between the two men got worse both in and out of the ring.

They first wrestled in a 1990 tag team match. Hart was part of the Hart Foundation. Michaels wrestled with the Rockers. In 1996, he defeated Hart in a 60-minute Iron Man match at WrestleMania.

Their final match was at Survivor Series in 1997. Michaels won the match and the World Heavyweight title when a questionable call was made.

In 2004, a disagreement between Matt Hardy and Edge led to Hardy being fired from WWE. Fans were furious, though, and Hardy soon returned to the company. The two wrestlers continued their feud.

At SummerSlam 2005, Edge defeated Hardy by dropping him onto a ringpost. The next month, Hardy defeated Edge in a steel cage match. A few weeks later, the wrestlers tried to settle the feud in a Loser Leaves *Raw* ladder match. Hardy's former wrestling partner Lita helped Edge defeat Hardy. Hardy then left to wrestle on the *SmackDown* TV show.

Family, Fame, and Fortune

Family Ties

Watching wrestling is an activity many families enjoy together. But did you know that some families also make their living by wrestling? Several of today's wrestlers have fathers, brothers, uncles, and even grandfathers in the wrestling business.

Calgary, Alberta, Canada, is the home of a famous wrestling family. Stu Hart opened a wrestling school in his basement in the late 1940s. Hart trained all eight of his sons and several other relatives at his school. Two of his sons, Bret and Owen, became WWE superstars.

FACT: Stu Hart's school is nicknamed "The Dungeon."

Fritz Von Erich started his own wrestling company in Dallas, Texas. He called it World Class Championship Wrestling (WCCW). Five of his sons—Kerry, Kevin, Mike, David, and Chris—followed him into the wrestling business.

THE VON ERICHS

Fritz • David • Kerry • Mike • Kevin • Chris

Kerry was the most popular of the brothers. He wrestled in both WCCW and the NWA before joining WWE in 1990. He left WWE in 1992. He died a year later. Tragically, Mike, David, and Chris also died at young ages. Today Kerry's daughter Lacey carries on the Von Erich tradition in Total Nonstop Action Wrestling.

The Royals of Wrestling

If the wrestling business had a royal family, it would be the McMahons. The family has been in the wrestling business for nearly 100 years.

In the early 1900s, Roderick "Jess" McMahon started promoting boxing matches at Madison Square Garden. By 1925, he was putting on pro wrestling shows in the northeastern United States. When Jess died in 1954, his son Vincent J. McMahon took over the business. Vince formed the World Wide Wrestling Federation (WWWF), which later became the WWF and is now WWE. In 1971, his son Vincent K. McMahon joined him in the business.

Vince bought the business from his father in 1982 and started moving the company's shows into other territories. He used cable TV to bring his shows to the nation. WWE quickly became the biggest wrestling company in the country. In the early 2000s, the company bought World Championship Wrestling (WCW) and Extreme Championship Wrestling (ECW).

Vince's wife, Linda, and their children, Shane and Stephanie, also have worked for WWE. Shane wrestled for the WWE. Stephanie has appeared on WWE TV shows. She was even briefly the Women's Champion! Stephanie's husband is top WWE wrestler Triple H.

McMahon Family Tree

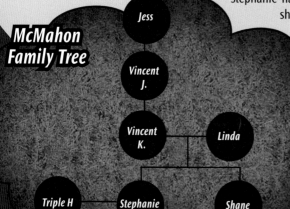

Jess

Vincent J.

Vincent K. — Linda

Triple H — Stephanie — Shane

The McMahons may be the most famous family in wrestling. However, many other families also have long histories in the sport. Among them are the Ortons, the DiBiases, the Smiths, the Maivias, and the Guerreros.

DiBiase Family Tree

Mike — Helen

Ted

Ted Jr.

Orton Family Tree

Bob Sr.

Cowboy Bob — Barry O

Randy

Maivia Family Tree

Peter Maivia

Rocky Johnson

The Rock

Smith Family Tree

Grizzly Smith

Jake Roberts — Sam Houston — Rockin' Robin

Guerrero Family Tree

Gory

Eddie — Hector — Mando — Chavo Sr.

Chavo Jr.

Climbing the Ladder to Success

Not all wrestlers have an easy climb to fame and fortune. For many, the superstar lifestyles they live now are very different from the way they grew up. But their hard work and their belief in their abilities helped them reach the top of their profession.

FACT:

Batista's nickname is "The Animal."

Perhaps no one has had a harder climb than Dave Batista. He rose up out of poverty to become one of wrestling's biggest stars.

Today Batista is one of the most popular wrestlers in the world.

February 21, 2010 Batista defeats John Cena to earn the WWE Championship title.

2005 Batista wins his first World Heavyweight Championship with the WWE and is named Wrestler of the Year by *Pro Wrestling Illustrated*.

2003 Batista wins his first tag team title with Ric Flair.

2002 Batista starts wrestling with WWE.

2000 Despite being turned away by WCW, Batista knows he can make it as a wrestler. He begins his career with Ohio Valley Wrestling (OVW). With OVW, he wins the Heavyweight Championship.

1986 Though he is only 17, Batista is living on his own. In time, he becomes a bouncer. He is arrested after two customers are hurt in a fight at the club where Batista works. Batista is sentenced to one year probation after the incident. He decides to become a bodybuilder.

1982 At 13, he is stealing cars.

January 18, 1969 David Michael Batista Jr. is born in Washington, D.C. His family is poor. They live in a rough neighborhood where murders aren't unusual.

Famous Outside the Ring

Once a wrestler reaches the top of the wrestling world, what's next?

From the Wrestling Arena to the Political Arena

Jesse "The Body" Ventura had an interesting career. After retiring from pro wrestling, he was elected mayor of his hometown, Brooklyn Park, Minnesota. He served as mayor from 1991 to 1995. Three years later, he ran for governor of Minnesota. He shocked the world by winning! Ventura served one term. Now he hosts radio and TV shows.

A Different Kind of Entertainment

In the 1980s and 1990s, Hulk Hogan took breaks from wrestling to make movies such as *Rocky III* and *Mr. Nanny*. From 2005 to 2007, he starred in a reality TV show, *Hogan Knows Best*.

Making Music

Chris Jericho turned his wrestling stardom and love of heavy-metal rock music into a part-time music career. He and his band, Fozzy, have recorded several CDs. Jericho also has acted in movies and appeared on TV shows.

The Rock is probably the most successful wrestler-turned-actor. He has starred in movies such as *Walking Tall*, *Race to Witch Mountain*, and *Planet 51*.

The Rock

FACT: Top WWE star John Cena seems ready to follow in The Rock's footsteps. He has starred in several action movies, including *The Marine* and *12 Rounds*. He also recorded a hip-hop CD.

Pro wrestling started in carnivals held in small towns. Today it's one of the biggest and most exciting entertainment businesses around. Where will wrestling go in the future? It's hard to say. But it seems likely that the fans will be right there, cheering on their favorite heroes and heels.

GLOSSARY

aerial move (AYR-ee-uhl MOOV)—a wrestling move that is done off the ropes or a high object, such as a ladder

babyface (BAY-bee-fayss)—a wrestler who acts as a hero in the ring

cruiserweight (KROOZ-ur-wayt)—a wrestling class in which wrestlers weigh no more than 215 pounds (97.5 kg)

feud (FYOOD)—a long-running quarrel between two people or groups of people

finishing move (FIN-ish-ing MOOV)—the move for which a wrestler is best known; this move also is called a signature move

gimmick (GIM-ik)—a clever trick or idea used to get people's attention

heel (HEEL)—a wrestler who acts as a villain in the ring

pay-per-view (PAY PUR VYOO)—a cable or satellite TV service that allows customers to watch special events for a fee

promoter (pruh-MOH-tur)—a person or company that puts on a sporting event

referee (ref-uh-REE)—a person at a sports event who makes participants obey the rules

stable (STAY-buhl)—a group of wrestlers who protect one another during matches and sometimes wrestle together

territory (TER-uh-tor-ee)—an area controlled by one wrestling promoter

valet (vah-LAY)—a person who walks to the ring with a wrestler and helps the wrestler during matches

READ MORE

Kaelberer, Angie Peterson. *The McMahons: Vince McMahon and Family.* Mankato, Minn.: Capstone Press, 2004.

O'Shei, Tim. *Batista.* Mankato, Minn.: Capstone Press, 2010.

O'Shei, Tim. *Undertaker.* Mankato, Minn.: Capstone Press, 2010.

Price, Sean. *Chris Jericho.* Mankato, Minn.: Capstone Press, 2010.

Shields, Brian, and Kevin Sullivan. *WWE Encyclopedia: The Definitive Guide to World Wrestling Entertainment.* New York: DK Publishing, 2009.

INTERNET SITES

FactHound offers a safe, fun way to find Internet sites related to this book. All of the sites on FactHound have been researched by our staff.

Here's all you do:

Visit *www.facthound.com*

Type in this code: **9781429647892**

American Wrestling Association
  (AWA), 9, 29
Andre the Giant, 24, 26
Austin, "Stone Cold" Steve, 15, 16

Batista, David Michael, Jr., 42–43

catchphrases, 12, 15
Cena, John, 4, 19, 43, 45
characters, 12–13, 14–15
Chyna, 16, 31, 34
costumes, 12, 13, 14, 23

Edge, 4, 11, 18, 37
Extreme Championship Wrestling
  (ECW), 30, 40

families, 30, 38–39, 40–41
feuds, 36–37
finishing moves, 20, 21, 27, 30

gimmick matches, 16–17,
  18–19, 27, 34, 37
Gonzales, Jorge "Giant," 23
Gorgeous George, 7, 12–13

Hardy, Matt, 4, 11, 22, 30, 37
Hart, Bret "Hitman," 15, 27,
  37, 38
Hogan, "Hollywood" Hulk, 15,
  24, 26, 31, 36, 44
Hornswoggle, 22

Jericho, Chris, 4, 11, 18, 21, 44

Kane, 8, 11, 15, 18

McMahon, Vincent J., 40

Michaels, Shawn, 4, 27, 29,
  31, 37
movies, 44, 45

National Wrestling Alliance
  (NWA), 9, 32, 33, 39

politics, 5, 44

Roberts, Jake "The Snake,"
  13, 21, 41
The Rock, 8, 15, 41, 45
rules, 10–11, 16

Savage, "Macho Man" Randy,
  15, 36
stables, 28, 31

tag teams, 11, 15, 28, 29, 30,
  31, 36, 37, 43
television, 4, 6, 7, 8, 24, 25,
  37, 40, 44
territories, 8, 9, 40
Thesz, Lou, 7, 20
Total Nonstop Action Wrestling
  (TNA), 9, 39
Triple H, 4, 21, 31, 34, 40

Undertaker, 4, 8, 14–15, 17, 27

women, 32, 33, 34, 35, 40
World Championship Wrestling
  (WCW), 9, 31, 40, 43
World Wrestling Entertainment
  (WWE), 8, 9, 14, 16, 19, 22, 24
  25, 28, 29, 30, 31, 33, 34, 35,
  37, 38, 39, 40, 43, 45
WrestleMania, 4, 18, 24, 25, 26,
  27, 36, 37